VISIONARY POWER

The Power of a Successful Visionary

By Rickie Bowser

PRESS

CONTENTS

Chapter 1

Where There Is No Vision

Your vision, or how you view things, is very important for it determines your future. The way you see things in your present state is the way they are. Scripture tells us, **"As a man thinks in his heart, so is he" (Prov. 23:7)**. Life begins on the inside; the inside is the key to what is manifested on the outside, so the inside must change. Jesus said, **"What comes out of a man is what makes him 'unclean.' For from within, out of men's hearts, come evil thoughts, sexual immorality, theft, murder,**

adultery, greed, malice, deceit, lewdness, envy, slander, arrogance and folly. All these evils come from inside and make a man 'unclean'" (Mark 7:20-23).

Our lives are based on our vision of ourselves, for how we see ourselves is how we see others.

"And to love Him out of and with all the heart and with all the understanding [with the faculty of quick apprehension and intelligence and keenness of discernment] and with all the strength, and to love one's neighbor as oneself, is much more than all the whole burnt offerings and sacrifices" (Mark 12:33 Amp).

"Where there is no vision the people perish" (Prov. 29:18). Each life is a manifestation of the Word of life that is in it; life is the light of a man; how someone views his life is the way he views the Word that he has received. **"In Him was Life, and the Life was the Light of men. And the Light shines on in the darkness, for the darkness has never overpowered it [put it out or absorbed it or appropriated it, and is unreceptive to it]"** **(John 1:4-5)**.

Let me explain: the biblical character of Joseph was a special young man when it comes to visionary power. Why? Because of how he viewed present situations, something I will go into in great depth later in this book. Most people's vision is so shallow they can't see past their present situation; this ties us all together whether rich, poor, black, or white. It does not matter. We all suffer from the same problems, and those problems started with Adam and Eve—low self-esteem!

God created us at the highest level, and one word received from someone Adam and Eve didn't even know changed all that. With us one word from someone we do know causes us to doubt what God has said to us.

Then they told him, and said: "We went to the land where you sent us. It truly flows with milk and honey, and this *is* its fruit. Nevertheless the people who dwell in the land *are* strong; the cities *are* fortified *and* very large; moreover we saw the descendants of Anak there. The Amalekites dwell in the land of the South; the Hittites, the Jebusites, and the Amorites dwell in the mountains; and the Canaanites dwell by the sea and along the banks of the Jordan." Then Caleb quieted the people before Moses, and said, "Let us go up at once and take possession, for we are well able to overcome it." But the men who had gone up with him said, "We are not able to go up against the people, for they *are* stronger than we." And they gave the children of Israel a bad report of the land which they had spied out, saying, "The land through which we have gone as spies *is* a land that devours its inhabitants, and all the people whom we saw in it *are* men of *great* stature. There we saw the giants (the descendants of Anak came from the giants); and we were like grasshoppers in our own sight, and so we were in their sight."

Numbers 13: 27-33

Why did all this happen? Because we are dull of hearing; we would much rather listen to man than to the Word of God. Genesis 1:26-28 says,

> Then God said, "Let Us make man in Our image, according to Our likeness; let them have dominion over the fish of the sea, over the birds of the air, and over the cattle, over all the earth and over every creeping thing that creeps on the earth." So God created man in His *own* image; in the image of God He created him; male and female He created them. Then God blessed them, and God said to them, "Be fruitful and multiply; fill the earth and subdue it; have dominion over the fish of the sea, over the birds of the air, and over every living thing that moves on the earth. And God said, "See, I have given you every herb *that* yields seed which *is*

on the face of all the earth, and every tree whose fruit yields seed; to you it shall be for food."

Then God told them about the tree in the midst of the garden: "**Then the LORD God took the man and put him in the Garden of Eden to tend and keep it. And the LORD God commanded the man, saying, "Of every tree of the garden you may freely eat; but of the tree of the knowledge of good and evil you shall not eat, for in the day that you eat of it you shall surely die" (Gen. 2:15-17).** Why is it that we focus more on what we can't have than on what we can, and then look for someone to blame for its results? This was the first choice Adam and Eve made after acquiring the knowledge of good and evil, knowing that God said it would bring forth death; they chose it anyway.

Consequently we are still feeling the pressure of how we look; we are still making decisions blatantly disregarding the knowledge we have been given pertaining to life versus the knowledge of good and evil. Even though we have been freed from this curse, we still choose the knowledge of good and evil over life. How? By rejecting what God has said about us and by blaming others, blaming society, blaming the economy, and blaming even God Himself for our situations.

God commanded mankind to be fruitful and multiply, but that vision was tainted by self-righteousness. Self-righteousness is a spirit, and that spirit was received when man believed the word of the serpent over God, and to this day man still cannot see past himself because of that spirit of low self-esteem. This couple (Adam and Eve) was very successful, very wealthy, and had need of nothing; their future was based upon the word they had received from God in the beginning, so when Satan challenged the authenticity of that word, he challenged its origin—the One from whom the vision came. Once doubt is introduced and received into one's vision, the whole outcome of that vision is changed. When the seed of doubt is planted, everything produced from that seed will have doubt as part of its makeup.

Adam and Eve had two sons who were totally opposite from each other in spirit. Cain and Abel both belonged to the same family, and both were gifted in their own way. Both were hard workers, visionaries of success, but only one of them was a successful visionary. The other one had a problem with his ability to see the gift that was in him, and this was a direct result of the loss of truth in this family. Now, truth was still there, but the ability to see it was blocked. The parents never envisioned the effect their choice would have on their sons, nor how the results would affect their future and the future choices of their children's children. The gift of life was still there, but the desire to choose it was not.

The power to choose life was replaced with the desire to know good and evil, so the boys were left to make their own way. You know what happens when you leave children to themselves! These two brothers were no different. They were of the same seed, so no matter how they looked they couldn't change what was in them. The Lord in His wisdom founded the earth, and by His understanding He established the heavens. A person is destroyed for lack of knowledge. When knowledge is void of life, wisdom is absent and understanding is absent; therefore the ability to discern the place of origin is absent.

Let's apply this principle to our giving to the Lord. How you give and what you give will always reveal the source of your gift. The lack of a vision will always distort your giving, and you will find yourself going about to establish your own view of giving. So through the lack of knowledge, one brother killed the other because his worship, through his giving, was not received, and his brother's was.

Cain's murderous act destroyed his own future, and he blamed his brother for the result of what came out of his own heart. It wasn't his brother's fault that his worship to God was not received.

His own attitude, in his giving toward God, turned an incident into a permanent situation. Now don't get this wrong! Cain also had the opportunity to do what was right, but instead he chose to eliminate his example (Abel) rather than learn from him. This is something that man does even today; by speaking against things we don't understand, we seal our own fate.

Let me clarify some things for you. You will never master the knowledge of good and evil because it's not in you to do so. The will to do right is always present. Let me say that again: the will to do right is always present. But what often seems to escape us is the way to perform it.

Humility is the secret to a successful vision, and every vision has to have an appointed time, a time in which an individual chooses to be successful. Time is the process by which the vision is established, and every vision has a testing period. This is where most people fail! *They lack the ability to stand and watch.*

God stood and watched His vision, to see what it would say. When it was reproved, this became the testing time. Habakkuk was given the vision of God and the revelation by the Spirit that the vision was for an appointed time, and **"at the end, it shall speak, and not lie" (Hab. 2:3)**.

Time is divided into seasons. The season you are in determines the direction of your vision. In the garden, God tested the vision by asking Adam a couple of questions: 1) **"Where are you? 2) "Who told you?" (Gen. 3:9-11)**. Adam's answers determined God's next move, for God had already placed conse-quences upon His word, which He had given to man. Based upon man's choice, God had to separate Himself from Adam for a season. But He did not want to do so without giving Adam a chance to see what he had gained, and lost, through his decision.

Most people don't put restrictions on their visions, and this is one of the main reasons why their visions are not successful. Restrictions force you to keep your word and be true to your vision. This is the process of a truly successful visionary (being fully persuaded that neither height, nor depth, nor things seen, nor things not seen, nor any other thing shall be able to shake you from what is in your heart). The process is designed for true visionaries, and a true visionary knows the outcome. He is fully persuaded that nothing can or will separate him from the love that is the center of that vision.

You have to love what you do! God loves what He does! He saw it in His presence and lived it in the life of His creation. Man was created in the presence of God, in the image of God, and in the likeness of God!

Every vision has to be read entirely, but most people get so excited about something and take off running without having understood the process by which a successful vision is birthed. So halfway through the process, they quit! You must consider the process, because the process is inclusive to the outcome. Everything God made He declared good at the completion of it. He said "It is good" because He saw the end from the beginning and never lost sight of it. So I have some good news for you; it's finished! Do you believe that? We read in James 1:8, **"A double minded man is unstable in**

all his ways. Let not that man think that he shall receive anything."

A vision must be processed deep within the heart of the individual, but what sustains it is hope. **"Now faith is the substance of things hoped for, and the evidence of things not seen" (Heb. 11:1).** Hope that is seen is not hope, for why does a person hope for what he sees? But if a person hopes for what he does not see, then he waits for it with patience. Hope changes your future. Tying hope to your vision will change the way you see things.

God had hope for Adam and Eve, so He took responsibility for the state of their lives and gave them hope. He took responsibility and started making a way for their escape! Have you tried this with your children?

Love covers a multitude of sins and holds no record of wrong. You can't receive hope without understanding this. Hope is created by experience, and when hope is developed like this, a successful vision is created that causes you not to be ashamed of your present state, knowing that it is temporal.

There are men and women who were prostitutes, drug addicts, thieves, drunks, and liars whose lives were given hope because of what they heard. They believed, and if you can believe, you can see the glory of God! Some people think this applies only to these types of people, but I'm sorry, this means you too! You may have been raised in a Christian home and feel you are a morally good person, but you are in as much pain as one of them and need to believe that God your Father is for you. Not somebody else, but for you—your situation is temporal.

It does not matter what your life was or is like. It cannot change how He sees you. You might stop looking at Him as a Father, but He will never stop looking at you as His child. His vision of His love for you was, is, and always will be "I have to; My child needs me."

He understood that we would not come to Him, because of our state of being, because of our pride, so He came to us; He did not come to us to condemn us but that we through Him might be saved. That's why He makes this statement, **"There is, therefore, now no condemnation to those who are in Christ Jesus" (Rom. 8:1)**.

God's vision of restoration is beyond man's normal understanding of life, because the wisdom of God is a mystery to the natural man; man does not understand that God's love for him is so deep that when He made man, He purposely hid His Word in man, so that at an appointed time, if man would listen, he would hear the Father calling him, "Come out."

"But the eye has not seen, the ear has not heard, and neither has it entered into the heart of a man, the things which God has prepared for them that love Him" (1 Cor. 2:9). He loves you, but the question is, do you love Him? The spirit of a man will sustain him in sickness, but a broken spirit who can bear, who can stop the pain? They who are not sick do not need to be healed. They who are not weak do not need strength. Jesus said, **"I did not come to call the righteous, but sinners to repentance" (Matt. 9:13)**.

Faith is the substance required for this to happen, because there are so many things at work. The natural man cannot receive this because he does not know how to **"count it**

all joy" (James 1:2). So how can we relate that to someone in need? We can't. God, understanding the helplessness of a man, and the impossibility of his ever delivering himself, made Himself a sacrifice, and that sacrifice was His Son. For when He could not depend on anyone else, He depended on Himself! And for the joy set before Him, He endured the cross, despising the shame. Never losing sight of the vision of restoration, He created a pathway for man to be reconciled back to Him.

God was in Christ reconciling the world unto Himself, not imputing their trespasses unto them; and He has committed to us the word of reconciliation and the ministry of reconciliation. That is why **"if anyone be in Christ, he is a new creation; old things are passed away, and behold all things have become new, and all things are of God" (2 Cor. 5:17)**.

This is considered a successful vision. **"It is God who is at work in you; both to will, and to do of His good pleasure" (Phil. 2:13)**.

Train up a Child

God has a distinct teaching ability that He has passed on to us, and that is the ability to train. So often when we learn things, we learn them from the wrong people. **"Train up a child in the way he should go, and when he is old he will not depart from it" (Prov. 22:6 NKJV)**.

This process must be followed without exception, the reason being that all creation has been given this same ability. You are not telling them which way they should go, but you are training them.

You must understand what this means in order to understand the gift of training you have received and its importance. We all have some form of leadership we are following in this process, because we are not the first.

Luke 4:1-4 gives us a good example of this: **"Then Jesus, being filled with the Holy Spirit, returned from the Jordan and was led by the Spirit into the wilderness, being tempted for forty days by the devil. And in those days He ate nothing, and afterward, when they had ended, He was hungry. And the devil said to Him, 'If You are the Son of God, command this stone to become bread.' But Jesus answered him, saying, 'It is written, "Man shall not live by bread alone, but by every word of God."'"**

I find two keys in verse one: 1) He was filled; 2) He was led. Being filled and being led is such a vital combination of the natural and the spirit man's training that God is always willing to allow such tests to occur to perfect His will so that man will be like Him in every way. How did Jesus arrive at this stage in His natural life? There had to be some form of training on the natural level; we know there was on the spiritual level because God is a Spirit, so that's not in question. But the natural is in question, the reason being that man cannot receive the things of the Spirit, nor can he understand them, but man can receive the things of the natural.

Understanding the natural is vital to understanding the spiritual because God is a Spirit, and the closest man has been to seeing God is the person of Jesus Christ.

Man's fall was spiritual, but it was based on his natural decision. Therefore God needed to restore man's natural authority in order to restore his spiritual authority. Otherwise we could never hope to obtain this level of manifestation that we see exemplified in these verses in the person of Jesus Christ. So let's explore this training a little deeper.

Now so it was *that* after three days they found Him in the temple, sitting in the midst of the teachers, both listening to them and asking them questions. And all who heard Him were astonished at His understanding and answers. So when they saw Him, they were amazed; and His mother said to Him, "Son, why have You done this to us? Look, your father and I have sought You anxiously." And He said to them, "Why did you seek Me? Did you not know that I must be about My Father's business?" But they did not understand the statement which He spoke to them. Then He went down with them and came to Nazareth, and was subject to them, but His mother kept all these things in her heart. And Jesus increased in wisdom and stature, and in favor with God and men.

Luke 2:46-52

Know ye not, that to whom ye present yourselves as servants unto obedience, his servants ye are whom ye obey; whether of sin unto death, or of obedience unto righteousness? But thanks be to God, that, whereas ye were servants of sin, ye became obedient from the heart to that form of teaching whereunto ye were delivered; and being made free from sin, ye became servants of righteousness. I speak after the manner of men because of the infirmity of your flesh: for as ye presented your members as servants to uncleanness and to iniquity unto iniquity, even so now present your members as servants to righteousness unto sanctification. For when ye were servants of sin, ye were free in regard of righteousness. What fruit then had ye at that time in the things whereof ye are now ashamed? For the end of those things is death. But now being made free from sin and become servants to God, ye have your fruit unto sanctification, and the end eternal life.

Romans 6:16-22

Again, we see through these verses how deep this training is and how intense the process is! God is willing to go to great lengths to accomplish His will, because He understands that this gift has the ability to be used for good and for bad. Why? Because this gift is a manifestation of the words we hear and choose to submit to.

Jesus spoke these words, lifted up His eyes to heaven, and said: "Father, the hour has come. Glorify Your Son, that Your Son also may glorify You, as You have given Him authority over all flesh, that He should give eternal life to as many as You have given Him. And this is eternal life, that they may know You, the only true God, and Jesus Christ whom You have sent. I have glorified You on the earth. I have finished the work which You have given Me to do. And now, O Father, glorify Me together with Yourself, with the glory which I had with You before the world was. I have manifested your name to the men whom You have given Me out of the world. They were Yours, You gave them to me, and they have kept your word. Now they have known that all things which You have given Me are from You. For I have given to them the words which You have given Me; and they have received *them,* and have known surely that I came forth from You; and they have believed that You sent Me.

John 17:1-8

Training is not just talking; it is a manifestation of how we respond to what we hear about ourselves:

Behold what manner of love the Father has bestowed on us, that we should be called children of God! Therefore the world does not know us, because it did not know Him. Beloved, now are we the children of God; and it has not yet been revealed what we shall be, but we know that when He is revealed, we shall be like Him, for we shall see Him as He is. And everyone who has this hope in Him purifies himself, just as He is pure.

1 John 3:1-3

Manifestation is the result of what you deem to be true, and this is based on your living—the reason being if you're good you cannot manifest evil, and if you're evil you cannot manifest good.

1. **Matthew 3:10**: **"The ax is already at the root of the trees, and every tree that does not produce good fruit will be cut down and thrown into the fire."**

2. **Matthew 7:16-18**: **"By their fruit you will recognize them. Do people pick grapes from thorn bushes, or figs from thistles? Likewise every good tree bears good fruit, but a bad tree bears bad fruit. A good tree cannot bear bad fruit, and a bad tree cannot bear good fruit."**

3. Do you know why Jesus was manifested?

   And you know that He was manifested to take away our sins, and in Him there is no sin. Whoever abides in Him does not sin. Whoever sins has neither seen Him nor known Him. Little children, let no one deceive you. He who practices righteousness is righteous, just as He is righteous. He who sins is of the devil, for the devil has sinned from the beginning. For this purpose the Son of God was manifested, that He might destroy the works of the devil. Whoever has been born of God does not sin, for His seed remains in him; and he cannot sin, because he has been born of God.

1 John 3:5-9

4. **Matthew 7:18**: **"A good tree cannot bear bad fruit, and a bad tree cannot bear good fruit."**

5. **Matthew 7:19: "Every tree that does not bear good fruit is cut down and thrown into the fire."**

6. **Matthew 12:33: "Make a tree good and its fruit will be good, or make a tree bad and its fruit will be bad, for a tree is recognized by its fruit."**

For I consider that the sufferings of this present time are not worthy to be compared with the glory which shall be revealed in us. For the earnest expectation of the creation eagerly waits for the revealing of the sons of God. For the creation was subjected to futility, not willingly, but because of Him who subjected it in hope....

Romans 8:18-20

Visionaries are livers, and God is the biggest visionary of them all. Who else would subject His creation to such cruelty except God, who knows the end from the beginning? God is not caught up in the present but in the process. Last place I read, Satan's vision of himself was no good without reproduction. Without the ability to reproduce he could not carry out his desire to be like God. Now before I go on, where do you think Satan got this vision from? Reproduction is a distinct design of God; God did not discuss with Satan His plan to make man in His own image and likeness, He just did it. Somehow though Satan did receive this knowledge, so where did it come from? There is no recording of any reproduction having been done, just the knowledge that everything God made had this ability for it to be done.

I believe God used the tree of the knowledge of good and evil to spark an idea of His vision into the mind of Satan that knowledge combined with speaking was how this happened. God had already spoken everything into existence, and everything He said came to pass, so this had to be true. But was it the whole truth?

Truth is the indisputable fact that something has the actual character of being true, and since God made man from Himself, this must be the actual character of truth, and if man is the actual character of God, *If I can corrupt him through knowledge I can become truth, and everything will be under my control*, Satan thought.

How do we know this to be a fact?

Training took place immediately; his first pupil was the woman. He sowed into her a seed of rebellion. Through their conversation he discovered that she had an interest in the tree. A seed of disobedience was sown with man; this was more of a guess because Satan wasn't exactly sure how Adam would respond to his wife's decision.

Through his observation of man he noticed how man followed God's command to the letter. Again, he was not sure how this would work because man had not shown any desire other than that of an obedient son. Adam's acceptance of the fruit at the hand of his wife allowed the effects of deceit to produce seeds of disobedience in him. The results were evident immediately; Adam heard God walking in the garden, and for the first time his response was not joy but shame, all because he had received a word from someone other than God. This was bigger than even Satan could have imagined, because of his limited knowledge of God's will.

Howbeit we speak wisdom among them that are perfect: yet not the wisdom of this world, nor of the princes of this world, that comes to nothing: But we speak the wisdom of God in a mystery, even the hidden wisdom, which God ordained before the world unto our glory: Which none of the princes of this world knew: for had they known it, they would not have crucified the Lord of glory. But as it is written, Eye has not seen, nor ear heard, neither has it entered into the heart of man, the things which God has prepared for them that love him. But God has revealed them unto us by his Spirit: for the Spirit searches all things, yes, the deep things of God. For what man knows the things of a man, save the spirit of man which is in him? Even so the things of God know no man, but the Spirit of God. Now we have received, not the spirit of the world, but the Spirit who is from God, that we might know the things that have been freely given to us by God. Which things also we speak, not in the words which man's wisdom teaches, but which the Holy Ghost teaches; comparing spiritual things with spiritual. But the natural man receives not the things of the Spirit of God: for they are foolishness to him: neither can he know them, because they are spiritually discerned.

1 Corinthians 2:6-14 KJV

It is evident from the results of the fall that Satan had no knowledge of God's will; man's nakedness and shame were covered by God, and this very act was hidden from Satan by his own pride. God proceeded with the training up of His child in the way he should go so that at the appointed time he would manifest the characteristics of a son.

Important statement (don't ever forget it): pride will always blind you to the truth! Satan proceeded with his reproductive plan, misunderstanding God's reproductive plan. All this came to pass because man did not exercise dominion over the earth and subdue it, thereby becoming a willing participant in receiving the seed of disobedience. Don't take this the wrong way; this was not about the will of man or the will of the woman but about the will of God. God does not operate independently of Himself; He operates in unity with Himself, manifesting the Spirit of one in every aspect of His existence. Therefore God never intended for man or woman to operate independently of each other. So to clarify, by man's not taking authority in this situation over himself, he was making a statement that he and the woman were not one but individuals of God's creation with the ability to operate independently of each other, manifesting their own wills for themselves in a world designed to operate in unity.

God made man from the dust of the earth and put His Spirit in him, and man became a living soul. He proceeded to take a rib from man and create a woman, signifying His intentions of unity and reproduction that without each other they could not reproduce. God purposely reproduced Himself by putting authority in man and compassion in woman, making sure that unless the two became one He would not be complete in them, and they would struggle with the understanding of His existence in them. This is where we get the statement in Genesis 2:21-25:

And the LORD God caused a deep sleep to fall on Adam, and he slept; and He took one of his ribs, and closed up the flesh in its place. Then the rib which the LORD God had taken from man He made into a woman, and He brought her to the man. And Adam said: "This is now bone of my bones and flesh of my flesh; she shall be called Woman, because she was taken out of Man." Therefore a man shall leave his father and mother and be joined to his wife, and they shall become one flesh.

And they were both naked, the man and his wife, and were not ashamed.

This battle of wills took place first in heaven when Satan said, "I will be like the most high God."

God accepted the challenge knowing that He needed someone to help Him perfect His vision of Himself, and who better than the one He created for such a purpose. This was Satan's first training test for man, because he believed man was the key to being like God. Now, do you believe all this happened by itself? That is like believing there was a big bang, and—*boom!*—life emerged. Life on earth is not the result of some big bang; it is the result of the biggest visionary in the universe, God Himself.

Let me introduce you to Him, and the training up of His children, and the way they should go.

I believe sometimes when we read or hear something for the first time, we think it is something new. That is true and false: true because it's your first time; false because it already existed with God. You were just unable to hear it until now. Why? Only He knows. Training does not produce instant ability, it only produces instant knowledge, and instant knowledge does not produce instant change—time does that.

He came unto his own, and his own received him not. But as many as received him, to them gave he the power to become the sons of God, even to them that believe on his name: Which were born, not of blood, nor of the will of the flesh, nor of the will of man, but of God. And the Word was made flesh, and dwelt among us, (and we beheld his glory, the glory as of the only begotten of the Father,) full of grace and truth.

John 1:11-14

God is all about time; this is one of the main reasons why He created seasons. Seasons are the process of time, because time processes knowledge, and that knowledge produces opportunities by which abilities are manifested. Once abilities are manifested, seasons and times become important to the growth of those abilities.

Hebrews 5:14: "But solid food belongs to those who are of full age, that is, those who

by reason of use have their senses exercised to discern both good and evil."

Ephesians 6:4: "And you, fathers, do not provoke your children to wrath, but bring them up in the training and admonition of the Lord."

Romans 8:14-19: "For as many as are led by the Spirit of God, they are the sons of God. For ye have not received the spirit of bondage again to fear; but ye have received the Spirit of adoption, whereby we cry, Abba, Father. The Spirit itself bears witness with our spirit, that we are the children of God: And if children, then heirs; heirs of God, and joint-heirs with Christ; if so be that we suffer with him, that we may be also glorified together. For I reckon

that the sufferings of this present time are not worthy to be compared with the glory which shall be revealed in us. For the earnest expectation of the creature waits for the manifestation of the sons of God."

Who are you? John 14:10-13 gives the answer:

Do you not believe that I am in the Father, and that the Father is in Me? What I am telling you I do not say on My own authority and of My own accord; but the Father Who lives continually in Me does the (His) works (His own miracles, deeds of power). Believe Me that I am in the Father and the Father in Me; or else believe Me for the sake of the [very] works themselves. [If you cannot trust

Me, at least let these works that I do in My Father's name convince you.] I assure you, most solemnly I tell you, if anyone steadfastly believes in Me, he will himself be able to do the things that I do; and he will do even greater things than these, because I go to the Father. And I will do [I Myself will grant] whatever you ask in My Name [as presenting all that I AM], so that the Father may be glorified and extolled in (through) the Son. [Yes] I will grant [I Myself will do for you] whatever you shall ask in My Name [as presenting all that I AM].

What makes me a son? Read what 1 John 3:8-10 says:

He that commits sin is of the devil; for the devil sinned from the beginning. For this purpose the Son of God was manifested, that he might destroy the works of the devil. Who ever is born of God does not commit sin; for his seed remains in him, and he cannot sin, because he is born of God. In this the children of God are manifest, and the children of the devil: whosoever doeth not righteousness is not of God, neither he that loves not his brother.

And 1 Corinthians 4:14-16 (NKJV):

I do not write these things to shame you, but as my beloved children I warn *you.* For though you might have ten thousand instructors in Christ, yet *you do* not *have* many fathers; for in Christ Jesus I have begotten you through the gospel. Therefore I urge you, imitate me.

Chapter 2

What Do You See?

I want to tell you the story of a young man and his vision. In this story you will see and understand that **"as a person thinks in his heart, so is he" (Prov. 23:7)**, and it does not matter where he or she lives.

This young man grew up in Brooklyn, New York, in the '60s, when drugs and life were at the beginning stages of what you see now as a way of life. Every epidemic leaves a trail, and ours is quickly becoming a nation without God.

When this young man was growing up, street gangs and all sorts of organizations were vying for power and control. This young man was no different. He was learning from the generation before him that all things were possible to them that believed. Through this process he began to formulate his life without God, looking for his place of power, gaining knowledge, and learning that knowledge is power and without it man is destroyed. With it, he destroys those who lack power.

When this young man looked into his future, he saw the vision of what he wanted to be and where he wanted to go, but not how to get there. Faith and vision require that the doors of doubt and fear be shut. Vision was his hope, and through faith he took the action to fulfill it.

God has an amazing destiny for us! However, we have to make the right choices and walk in obedience to reach this destiny. How do you walk in obedience to someone you don't know? This young man was driven by purpose. That purpose was to escape being a statistic of the average young black man of his day—either dead, in prison, on a street corner dealing drugs, or using them and talking about what could have been.

Whether it's hidden talents, treasures, or ideas, you will find that God has already placed hope in your heart. He lights every man that comes into the world. When He says He came unto His own, that means you too! You may not know you belong to Him. This young man did not know his life was hid with Christ, but he was soon to find out. As his life began to take shape, drugs, alcohol, sex, sports, money, and materialism became his gods.

Life is a choice; life and death have been set before you. Choose life! How can you choose what you don't know? In Him is life, and that life is the Light of man. All that this young man did was in darkness, no matter how great the vision was for his future. The end was inevitable. "Apart from me," Jesus said, "you can do nothing." At the age of ten, this young man began to smoke pot, and by the time he was sixteen he started his own business. His desire for wealth increased. When he was twenty-one, he had five people working for him. He went to college at night full-time, but none of that was enough. By this time he was living a life well above his means, with no guidance, no wisdom, no knowledge, and no understanding of how to sustain his new lifestyle.

This young man's vision was almost full, almost accomplished. His goal was to be rich by the time he reached twenty-five. His destiny was set, or so he thought. But I'm here to tell you, **"there is a way which seems right to a man, but the end thereof are the ways of death" (Prov. 14:12)**. Right at the point of success, right at the point of human achievement, he discovered that all he had dreamed of had no fulfillment, no answer to what he was truly looking for. Neither money, drugs, friends, women, nor the hunger for more could fill the void, or the absence of God in his life. I was that young man!

All of our ways are clean in our own eyes, but God tries the spirit. Does this destroy the vision? I don't believe it does, because He who has begun a good work is able to perform it. God has begun a good work in man, and He will perfect it! The problem with most of us is letting Him do it!

How knowledgeable are you of God's redemptive power and that He prepared it for us before He made us? The average person lacks knowledge in this area, as I did. It is God who has predestined us. When God states, through the prophet Hosea, **"My people are destroyed for lack of knowledge" (Hosea 4:6)**, this is what he means! For whom He foreknew, He also predestined to be conformed to the image of His Son, but lack of knowledge of His Son is what destroys us. This is one of the greatest struggles in life. Everything in this life is designed to keep us from ever seeing what we were predestined by God to be.

When I understood that Jesus Christ came to seek and to save the lost, something happened inside of me; my spirit was released through the power of forgiveness. Forgiveness was predestined to succeed sin. That's why

"where sin increases, grace abounds all the more" (Rom. 5:20). The secret to forgiveness is in the way it is received. It was given unconditionally; it must also be received unconditionally. I know, you might ask, "How can it be that simple?" I thought, and then I tasted and saw that God was good. I asked for forgiveness, and I was changed; I confessed my sins before God and received God's forgiveness for sin, and now I am being changed from glory to glory! Can you see this? Have you changed your direction? This is what is known as repentance.

Chapter 3

Has It Been Revealed?

Forgiveness has to be revealed, and this too must come by way of vision. If a person can't see it, he can't receive it. Again, as stated in the previous chapter, **"where there is no vision, the people perish" (Prov. 29:18)**. You must be able to see yourself different from what you are, and the only way this can happen is if you will first **allow** yourself to be forgiven. Without this you will never see who you really are.

God did not send His Son to condemn you, but that through Him you might be saved. His desire is to reveal this to you in your spirit, but He can't get this information to you unless you first allow yourself to be forgiven.

God, understanding this need, planted forgiveness in the earth and let it grow up with us. He didn't just thrust it upon us but gradually walked us through it.

And at the appointed time, He revealed it through the death of His Son on the cross. This is why **"the preaching of the cross is to them that perish foolishness, but to us who are saved it is the power of God" (1 Cor. 1:18)**. And because we have received this, we have been changed. The same change we have received has been made available to everyone! When Jesus said **"Father, forgive them for they know not what they do"**

(Luke 23:24), He meant for this revelation to penetrate your spirit so that you can receive it.

The heart of man is being destroyed because of bitterness, because of unforgiveness. It is the goodness of the Lord that leads men to repentance. Good works don't get you to heaven, but **"faith without works is dead" (James 2:20)**.

In the previous chapters, we stated that **"eye has not seen nor ear heard, neither has it entered into the heart of man the things that God has prepared for them that love Him" (1 Cor. 2:9-10)**, but He has revealed them to us by His Spirit. For where the Spirit of the Lord is, there is liberty. Forgiveness can be received only in your spirit. Changing the inside of you will change the way you see on the outside.

The apostle Paul tells us, **"Nay, in all these things, we are more than conquerors"** **(Rom. 8:37)**. God is trying to implant this into our spirits, that even as He is, so are we in this world. Lift up your head! See your change! Then you will begin to live your change! For as a man thinks in his heart, so is he.

"He came that you may have life, and that you may have it more abundantly" (John 10:10). This is the revelation, the revealed truth! He is trying to get into your spirit because the words He speaks to us **are** Spirit and life! The flesh profits you nothing. That's why truth is revealed to your spirit, because your spirit is the control center of your flesh. So when your spirit is broken, your flesh is out of control, and all it knows is how it feels. This is why the breakdown of your spirit is uncontrollable, and no matter how hard you try to gain control, the more out-of-control your flesh becomes. The natural man cannot receive the things of the Spirit of God, neither can he know them, for they are spiritual and are spiritually discerned.

Your flesh will never be able to discern what your spirit needs!

Chapter 4

Spirit and Truth

I want to break down for you how to discern this. We start with the makeup of spirit and truth. The Holy Spirit exists as the vision by which man identifies with an invisible God. Truth exists as the testimony of an invisible God.

Let's begin. Where the Spirit of God is, there is liberty. Now, liberty is the existence of freedom. And freedom is the existence of life through the Spirit. Discerning this is important for a person to enjoy life in His Spirit. In the previous chapter, we explained that hope helps your vision. Now I want to express to you that through love your spirit can be free, and through your spirit you can receive hope for your future. You don't have to be perfect; just let Him perfect Himself in you and in your spirit. The Spirit of God quickens, for those who live according to the flesh set their minds on the things of the flesh, but those who live according to the Spirit, the things of the Spirit.

If the Spirit of Him who raised Jesus from the dead dwells in you, He who raised Christ from the dead will also give life to your mortal body through His Spirit who dwells in you. When you judge according to the flesh, you miss the testimony of God, which is the Truth He came to give you in your spirit. **"Now, the Lord is that Spirit, and where the Spirit of the Lord is, there is liberty. But we all, with unveiled**

faces, beholding as in a mirror the glory of the Lord, are being transformed into the same image from glory to glory, just as by the Spirit of the Lord" (2 Cor. 3:17–18), which calls those things which be not as though they were. Vision cannot be established without truth in the inward part of the body. Vision for others cannot be achieved; therefore vision for oneself also cannot be achieved. So let us establish the truth that is needed for this to happen. **"For you shall know the truth, and the truth shall make you free" (John 8:32).** Truth is the essence of being knowledgeable of things that have only a shadow of what is truth. Truth tries the very nature of one's ability to discern this.

When spirit and truth come together, worship is possible, for we cannot worship God except in spirit and in truth. The manifestation of the truth commends us to every man's con-science. But if this is hid, it is hidden to those who are perishing through the lack of this manifestation of truth, due to their inability to discern God's purpose. God's treasure, which is hidden in this earthly body, can only be revealed through truth, that the power may be of God and not of us.

"However, when He, the Spirit of Truth, has come, He will guide you into all truth. For He will not speak on His own authority, but whatever He hears He will speak and tell you things to come. He will glorify me; for he will take of what is mine and declare it to you" (John 16:13-14).

Who is he who overcomes the world but he who believes that Jesus is the Son of God? This is He who came by water and blood, and it is the Spirit who bears witness, because the

Spirit is truth. So you can't have one without the other. Consider what I say, and may the Lord give you understanding in all things, and the ability to discern.

Predestined to Succeed

God predestined His Word in you and me to succeed. Our destination is predetermined by His Word, so whatever word we join ourselves to, that is our destination. Why? Because it has already been predestined. (**Predestination is something that has been predetermined. In our case the world and the lives we live have been predetermined by God, so how does one man fail and another succeed? By choosing either what God has predetermined, for success, or failure.**)

Succeed: to follow or replace another by descent, election, appointment, etc. To come next after something else in an order or series.

Success: the favorable or prosperous termination of attempts or endeavors.

Failure: an act or instance of failing or proving unsuccessful; lack of success: *His effort ended in failure. The campaign was a failure.*

God has either predestined that word for success or failure; you have only to choose. **"And if it seems evil to you to serve the LORD, choose for yourselves this day whom you will serve, whether the gods which your fathers served that *were* on the other side of the River, or the gods of the Amorites, in whose land you dwell. But as for me and**

my house, we will serve the LORD" (Josh. 24:15 NKJV).

Whoever you choose to serve, you are calling them lord. You have nothing to do with the outcome of it, because the only thing you are lord of is your choice, and your only job is to choose. God planned its destination before the foundation of the world. I have good news for you though: you were predestined for success, but if you should find yourself entangled in failure, know that God has also predestined a way for you to escape by providing repentance—something Adam did not know in the garden. He had a chance to get out, but just as it was in the beginning, "you have to choose."

I have discovered that God's plan for man is for him to be successful, but the thing I want to show you more than anything is that you were predestined to succeed in him.

Let me give you a few more definitions to help you understand this fact. Some of them were already given, but I believe these definitions will help you understand God's will for you to be successful. Most people, when they hear this word *successful*, think immediately of money. What many people don't know is that money is a byproduct of success, a secondary or incidental product, as in a process of manufacture, the result of another action, often unforeseen or unintended.

Let's get back to the book.

Predestined: **1.** to fix upon, decide, or decree in ADVANCE; FOREORDAINED **2.** *Theology* To fore-ordain or elect by divine will or decree.

Advance: **1.** to accelerate the growth or progress of **2.** to bring or move forward **3.** to rise to a higher rank **4.** to lift up: raise **5.** to bring forward in time; *especially* to make earlier **6.** to bring forward for notice, consideration, or acceptance.

Foreordained: to dispose or appoint in advance.

Succeed: **1a.** to come next after another in office or position or in possession of an estate; *especially* to inherit sovereignty, rank, or title **b.** to follow after another in order **2a.** to turn out well **b.** to attain a desired object or end <students who *succeed* in college> **3** *obsolete*: to pass to a person by inheritance (*transitive* verb) **1.** to follow in sequence and especially immediately **2.** to come after as heir or successor.

God had always planned on showing us how to live a sin-free life; do you believe this? If so, then you believe already that we were predestined to succeed because to predestine means to decree in advance, and to succeed means to come after. **"The priest who is anointed and ordained to succeed his father as high priest is to make atonement. He is to put on the sacred linen garments"** (Lev. 16:32).

"I assure you, most solemnly I tell you, if anyone steadfastly believes in Me, he will himself be able to do the things that I do; and he will do even greater things than these, because I go to the Father" (John 14:12).

First Corinthians 15:45-49 states, **"The first man Adam became a living being. The last Adam became a life-giving spirit. However, the spiritual is not first, but the natural, and afterward the spiritual. The first man was of the earth, made of dust; the second Man is the Lord from heaven. As was the man of dust, so also are those who are made of**

dust; and as is the heavenly Man, so also are those who are heavenly. And as we have borne the image of the man of dust, we shall also bear the image of the heavenly Man."

God predestined man to be like Himself; everything in man is a process of elimination, so only that which is of God shall remain.

Now you could possibly ask the question, "How is this possible, seeing as God made everything?" Good question, and one that deserves an answer. Let us approach this with an answer that I believe God Himself is best qualified to give.

"The Lord has made everything [to accommodate itself and contribute] to its own end and His own purpose—even the wicked [are fitted for their role] for the day of calamity and evil" (Prov. 14:4 (Amp).

God has always had a purpose; that is why the Bible says in the beginning was the **Word**, because predestination is predetermined by the Word given by God to determine the destination of everything in existence. Predetermined: what does that mean? Exactly what it says; everything in life has already been predetermined. So again, what does that mean to you?

Predetermined: to settle, to ordain or decide in advance: (used with objective).

The only thing that determines your destination is your choosing to stay in that which has already been predetermined, and after this happens your future is predestined.

You are where you are because of what you heard and believed to be true; that was the only thing you had the power to do. Everything else was dictated before you chose what it would do in this process. Again, the only thing God gave you control of is your choice. You don't have to stay where you are; your leaving or staying does not dictate or change that which was predestined, because that which was pre-determined was not your doing but God's. But your choice does determine which one you will experience.

The destination of my choice has been predetermined, and not only was it predetermined, but the speed by which that choice is made determines placement in that destination according to availability. The only thing in life that is not determined by speed is salvation. Salvation is predestined by time, and that time is your lifetime. If you choose it before you die, it has been predetermined that you should be saved, and if not, it has been predetermined; I will let you figure that one out.

John 1:1-12: all the promises of God in our life were with Him in the beginning, and not one promise was not there. Our lives from the beginning were set up by God, by His Word, to be successful no matter what my choice was. That will never change. My belief in the Word that God set before me is the key. The beginning of success or failure is the Word. Why? Because without the Word nothing that exists would exist; what is God's definition of failure? Choice. When man chose the thing that God said would kill him, he defined failure. Why? Because failure can only be defined when a person leaves the path of success to explore the doubts and fears that occur because of uncertainties. Where do uncertainties come from? Uncertainties come from words of doubt and fear spoken against words of success and received as truth. What is God's definition of success? Submission (James 4:7). Visions of success were created in us when we were born, but the vision was without form—it was void, and darkness was upon the face of the deep, and the Spirit of God was moving on the face of the earth. Why? Waiting for a Word of life to be spoken, because in the Word is life, and that life is the light of man (John 1:4).

In order for man to be successful, light and darkness have to be separated. So what really happened in Genesis 3:1-11? The light was reunited with darkness, and man became confused about who he was. **Who are you? Do you know?** Jesus said He is the Light of the world, and then He turned to man and said he was the light of the world. So abortion is *nothing more than Satan trying to destroy the Light of the world, which is the Word of God*, in hopes that only darkness would exist, because in the beginning God separated them.

So when Jesus came His sole purpose was to separate the light from the darkness in the spirit realm once and for all. So guess what? It had nothing to do with you but everything to do with what was inside of you.

When the Scripture said He called you out of darkness into His marvelous light, this is what He was referring to (Rom. 8:1-3). What we were weak to do in the flesh, such as dying to sin and separating light from darkness, God sent His own Son in the likeness of sinful flesh to do what we were weak to do.

That is why Jesus said in John 14:30-31 that "the prince of this world comes and finds nothing in Me." The Word is the only thing that can separate the light from darkness, but before it can do that the Word of life has to be spoken so that the Spirit has something to work with. In Genesis 3:1, Eve received the seed of the serpent, which was his word over God's, and Adam did not reject it. That seed became the makeup of their family. If two people can agree in anything, nothing shall be impossible for them; God did not send His Son for man to stay in his sin: **"Pressing toward the mark of the high calling of God in Christ Jesus..."** **(Phil. 3:14)**. My mark has been set by God, and it's a high calling. I can't enter it without forgetting what's behind: my failures, my successes, everything. Second Corinthians 5:17-21 tells me that old things are passed away; God said behold all things have become new—all things. It has been predetermined that if you listen you will learn. It has also been predetermined that if you use what you have learned you will be successful.

Predestination is that which is known before a person chooses to learn; their choices determine the outcome they will experience, but it does not determine the destination, because the destination was predetermined by its maker.

Chapter 5

God Is

God is the author and finisher of our faith; therefore God is the maker of the Word, and in order to experience a successful vision one needs to know that God is. God is a very present help in times of trouble.

Let us begin to explore this fact that "God is." One of the first things I want to explore with you is that God is no respecter of persons when it comes to His Word (Is. 55:8-11). He does not think about or see things the way we do. A person has to perceive this in his spirit; a successful vision cannot be achieved without this.

The greatest revelation of this is that God is love. We always find ourselves struggling with this fact because of our need to please others. We are commanded to be imitators of God as dear children, and walk in love as Christ also has loved us and given Himself for us.

Now, may the God of peace, who brought up our Lord Jesus from the dead, make you complete in every good work to do His will, working in you what is well pleasing in His sight, through Jesus Christ, to whom is glory forever and ever. **(Heb. 13:20, 21)**

Let your conduct be without covetousness. Be content with such things as you have, for He Himself has said, **"I will never leave you nor forsake you" (Heb. 13:5)**. The purpose of this is so you may boldly say, **"The Lord is** my Helper; I will not fear. What can man do to me?" (Heb. 13:6). Being content does not mean sitting on the couch waiting for somebody else to do something, for all things are possible to them that believe God is.

"For the word of God is living, and powerful" (Heb. 4:12). Vision must have confidence, it must have boldness, it must have power, and above all it must have purpose.

None of these things can be achieved without the Word of God. Knowing that *God is* should create in you a confidence, for the Son of Man did not come to destroy men's lives but to save them. Truly the harvest is plentiful, but the laborers are few.

Surely God is in this place, and we did not know it! How does a person build his confidence? By believing that God is, and not only that He is, but that He is in this place. When a person gets a hold of this, and this word gets down in his spirit, nothing shall be impossible to him. Now that's confidence, knowing that you **"can do all things through Christ who strengthens me" (Phil. 4:13)**.

If people would do the best with their lives, finding out what God is doing in their generation and flinging themselves into it, they would discover that God is most glorified in them when they are most satisfied in Him.

When a person is able to bring God into his present situation by saying *God is*, something happens on the inside that words can't explain. The word *is* and the word *now* are so synonymous with a successful vision. Everything in our life appears to be such a struggle! Then He steps in and says, "Let's go out!" Most people's response to that is, "I've already tried it." And all they see is their past, while God is trying to get into their future. In your future is your successful vision, but the only way to get there is by going through your *now* into your *is.* Unless a person discovers the *God is* factor of their situation, it will never change. God never intended for man to fail. Because He has a strong desire to be believed, and goes through great lengths to make this happen. Is this for him? No. He will go to great lengths to get this into your spirit. He will even allow you to continue in your present situation until you say, "God is! This is not who I am; I don't understand why this is happening, but I do understand that God is! And now my *is* has become *I am!* Now that *I am,* I have become more than a conqueror through Him."

Chapter 6

The Power to Become

Faith in the Word gives you the power to become successful in your vision. The first thing a person must determine is what he wants to become, and then he must hear it. People have always pressed upon the Word to hear what it would say to them. Remember, faith is still the substance of things hoped for, and the evidence of things not seen; faith still comes only by hearing, and hearing by the Word of God. The power to become a successful visionary hinges on the evidence produced from our hearing through our pressing, and then it becomes our *now*. Once faith becomes *now*, it has crossed into the realm of substance, and once it becomes substance you have something you can handle. Jesus said to the disciples after His resurrection, when He appeared to them in the room, **"Handle me, and see, for spirits don't have flesh and bones" (Luke 24:39)**.

Can you hear the "power to become" speaking to you? Most people need substance to become, but that person who can hear and become is in another realm altogether. Such a person is motivated by his faith, not his sight. Therefore, he is a mountain mover, not a mountain watcher. Mountain movers conquer doubt because they know doubt hinders them from achieving their potential, and faith helps them. Doubt says, "It's impossible." Faith says,

"I can do all things through Christ." You must recognize your thought source so that you can realize "as you are thinking in your heart, so are you." Without this proper knowledge, your every move is based on feelings and not on faith, and doubt once again takes over as your thought source.

When we are addressing the "power to become," we are addressing the source of how this happens. Until this can be unlocked within a person, everything is material, and so faith that comes by hearing is not heard. In the beginning is the Word, and the Word is with God. We need to discover our God beginning.

The Word gives us the power to begin, so let's take it to the next level. The Word all by itself produces life and death. When the Word is introduced into any situation it changes it, just by its very existence. The Word will occupy whatever space it is placed in. Nothing can stop the Word from living because it's alive all by itself. This is what the world has come to know as "seedtime and harvest."

Every seed sown bears seed of its own kind. The Word is the same as a seed. The Word can never fail to produce life and death. The moment the Word is spoken into existence, something dies, and the life of that spoken Word takes its place. There is nothing on the earth, under the earth, or above the earth with the power that the Word has of producing. So when we begin to understand the great gift that was given to us by God, and how important it is to our success and failure in life, we realize that God has given us everything pertaining unto life and godliness, through the power of the spoken Word. This is what He means when

He says, **"Death and life are in the power of the tongue" (Prov. 18:21)**.

The manifestation of the Word, spoken out of our mouths, will always result in change. Are you ready for change? Then speak the Word.

Chapter 7

Speak the Word Only

Do you have what it takes to believe in the authority of the Word, and is it enough to move you?

Let's address this issue of authority. Only a true servant of the Word can understand the power behind the authority given to speak the Word, because they themselves are under the authority of the Word and understand that this is how one moves in the realm of being a successful visionary. Also, they have come to understand that the greatest leader is also the greatest follower. The greatest leaders in every profession have learned to be good at what they do by being good at following what those who have gone before them have laid as a foundation to build on.

Let's talk about some foundational things; what is the foundation of what you believe? Do you speak the Word only? Is it based on truth? What do you speak? **"Out of the abundance of the heart the mouth speaks" (Matt. 12:34)**. This is where you lay your foundation. The heart is the focus of God's foundation, because out of your heart comes the issues of life. Basically what He's saying is give me your heart, and I will establish your goings. Whatever your vision of success is, it must have your heart, because there is no other successful foundation laid than that which God has laid, and that is Christ. Every successful vision is laid in God. How you build on this foundation determines the level of your success. The disciples of Jesus said, **"We cannot but speak the things that we have seen and heard of Him" (Acts: 4:20)**. And because they spoke the Word only, the manifestation of what they believed was evident to all who heard and believed, and the Lord added to them daily such as should be saved.

Speaking the Word only was the result of the disciples following Jesus and examining the authority by which He spoke the Word, and not only the authority, but also the power. The Word spoken by Jesus had power! Do you know your words have power? Until you discover that, the negative word will always overpower the positive Word, because it's easier for you not to believe! This is why the examples we follow are so important. Let me give you a couple of examples. The first man, Adam, was an example of negative living and negative speaking; therefore everyone who followed his example experienced the same results. Jesus was an example of positive living and positive speaking; therefore everyone who followed Him had the same results, because He followed the Father, and His results were the same as the Father's.

You cannot have one without the other! Positive living and positive speaking will always result in positive growth, because it is based on truth. You can't allow just anybody to speak into your life, because some things are detrimental to your spirit, even though they may have the appearance of truth. Some words are designed in the pit of hell to keep you from ever discovering your potential to be a successful visionary. Jesus said, **"You will know**

the truth, and the truth will make you free" **(John 8:32)**. When a person speaks into your life, it should free you. If it's from God, it should propel you forward. If not, it will bind you up and hinder you from ever moving into your potential for Christ. Jesus not only sets you free from sin, but because He is the spoken Word of God, and the living Word of God, He imparts to those who believe the example of how the living Word is based on truth, and truth is found in the heart of man. How a man lives and how a man speaks is a direct result of what's in his heart. If a man's heart is over-powered by lies, then every word he speaks and everything he does results in death. But if a man's life is overpowered by truth, then every word he speaks and everything he does will result in life, and life more abundantly, because **"in Him (in Truth) was life, and that life was the light of man" (John 1:4)**.

Speaking the Word only, watching it change the way you envision things, and seeing the results it produces in those who see how it transforms your life should motivate you. The spoken Word is what empowers a successful visionary, because **"out of the abundance of the heart the mouth speaks" (Matt. 12:34)**. What you speak is a direct predictor of what you will see in your future.

"Speaking the Word only" means speaking God only, trusting God only, allowing God only to speak into your life, so that He can trust you to speak into the life of others.

Things will begin to happen to prevent you from moving into this, because the god of this world knows that his time is short. Everyone who has God's hope in him will begin to purify himself through the spoken Word. Jesus said, **"Now you are clean through the Word I have spoken to you" (John 15:3)**, and since **"we have the same spirit of faith, according as it is written, 'I believed, there-fore have I spoken' [Ps. 116:10], we also believe and therefore speak, knowing that He who raised up the Lord Jesus will also raise us up with Jesus, and will present us with you" (2 Cor. 4:14).** For all things are for your sake! Don't let anything, or anyone, speak anything different from what the Word has spoken to you, **"that the abundant grace might through the thanksgiving of many abound to the glory of God" (2 Cor. 4:15).**

Chapter 8

The Anointing Destroys

This last chapter will address the need to be saved, and how this is achieved through the spoken Word, as described in the last couple of chapters.

David was in the field watching his father's sheep, and the prophet Samuel came to his house to anoint the next king of Israel (1 Samuel 16). All his brothers were there, but because David did not look like king material he was not called. I want to take this time to impart to you a little knowledge: *every opportunity to obey authority puts you in position to be blessed.* David was in position. He didn't leave the sheep and go home to see why the prophet was there, because he was too busy doing what his father had given him to do. Are you about the Father's business? So when the prophet tried to anoint one of those who were in the house, the Spirit of God within him sensed that God had not chosen any of them. He asked if someone was missing, because he knew he came there with the purpose of anointing the next king of Israel.

Jesse, David's father, responded, "I have one more son, but he's in the field watching the sheep." There was no glamour in watching sheep. The prophet responded, "We cannot go any further until he's called." The moment David came into the room, the Spirit of God moved on the prophet, and he said, "This is the one!" David's obedience to his father's spoken word positioned him to be seen by God.

Every part of us needs to be positioned for salvation, no exceptions. Most people get saved but never discipled, so they never get to experience the level of salvation the anointed Word brings to the whole body, because they move out of position. David received the anointing from the prophet and stayed in position to receive his next anointed Word. The word came to Jesse, the father of David, from the king that was being tormented by a spirit of distress, that he had a son who was skillful in playing the harp, a mighty man of valor, a man of war, prudent in speech, and the Lord was with him and he was with the sheep (1 Samuel 16). If a person allows the Word to position them for greatness through obedience, it is heard at the highest level.

David's obedience repositioned him into the battle of spiritual warfare, and because of the anointing that was on his life, he was able to bring peace to a tormented king (1 Samuel 16). This anointing not only brought peace to a tormented king, but also courage to a discouraged army (1 Samuel 17). The Philistines and their warrior Goliath were looking for a fight and challenged anyone who had the courage and the heart to come down and face him. Fear gripped the hearts of the people as well as their king, and their vision of success was blurred by fear.

This same David, because of his obedience to authority, was in position again to be used by God for His glory. When David rehearsed to God's people the success he had in watching his father's sheep, and protecting them from wild animals, their hearts were greatly strengthened. Their fear was replaced with courage when they saw his enthusiasm for God's vision of success (2 Samuel 17).

God always anoints a man to be used to destroy the yoke through obedience, because it's through the spoken Word that this happens. Moses, for example, responded to this call of God by saying, **"I am not eloquent enough to speak; I'm slow" (Ex. 4:10)**. God said, **"Who has made man's mouth? Or who makes the mute, the deaf, the seeing, or the blind? Have not I, the Lord? Now, therefore, go, and I will be your mouth, and teach you what you shall say" (Ex. 4:11)**. Obedience in Pharaoh's house positioned Moses for greatness in man's eyes, but obedience to the vision of God positioned him for greatness in God's house.

Here are a couple more examples of godly men serving ungodly people in the natural, but God in the Spirit.

Nehemiah's faithfulness in the service of an ungodly king positioned him for greatness and favor during a time when it was not popular to be an Israelite (Neh. 2:2-8). He received help to do the work of God to fulfill the vision for rebuilding the wall. Obedience to the king gave him the power to have a successful vision and positioned him to be a blessing to those who were also in position through obedience to have a successful vision (Nehemiah 3).

Daniel, another young man living in a time when most young men were being converted to ungodliness through the process of conformity, purposed in his heart to take a stand for the vision he had of greatness in his spirit (Dan. 1:1-8). He obeyed those who were in authority over him, but not to the point of disobeying God, and he was recognized as being ten times wiser and more understanding than those who had been conformed. He positioned himself and those with him for greatness (Dan. 1:11-20).

Joseph's level of visionary power is amazing considering that God positioned him for greatness with it, and he was propelled into position to discover the power of a successful visionary through obedience. The way you view every present situation you find yourself in makes the difference; every situation Joseph was in was used to bring glory to God, from the pit, to slavery, to prison, and eventually to destiny. The coat of many colors was used to put him in the pit, the pit was used to put him in slavery, where he found himself in the service of Potiphar, an ungodly man, a captain of Pharaoh's army, who recognized that the Lord was with Joseph (Gen. 39:1-5).

Joseph recognized the position he was in and purposed in his heart to obey the Word of God and the authority of the house over the temptation of his flesh. When he was tempted by Potiphar's wife to have sex, he resisted, was accused falsely, and imprisoned, but because of his obedience to the Word, he found himself in a position of favor once again (Gen. 40:41). As it was with David, Nehemiah, Daniel, and Joseph, so is it with all those who position themselves through obedience. The word of your gift travels; a man's gift will make room for him and bring him before great men (Prov. 18:18). So that you don't think this is only about men, let me tell you of some women who have walked in this level of obedience and were propelled into destiny through the power of being a successful visionary.

Ruth was an ungodly woman who married a man from a godly family, and through her obedience to the marriage covenant, even after her husband died, she entered into a covenant with her mother in-law, and with God, by faith (Ruth 1:17). Through obedience, she was willing to forsake all to follow the God of Naomi. Because of this and her willingness to walk in this level of obedience, she was miraculously propelled into the successful vision of God. Naomi instructed her to position herself to be noticed by Boaz, and what to do when she was noticed. When Boaz saw her, he was intrigued by the level of humility she exemplified and the anointing that was on her through her obedience to someone else's vision of success (Ruth 3).

Rehab the harlot saw the vision of God when she heard what He did for the Israelites in Egypt and was determined not to miss her opportunity to be blessed. She had a vision of her whole household being saved when she said to the two spies, **"Since I have shown you kindness, show me kindness and give me a true token, and spare my father, and my mother, my brothers, my sisters, and all that they have, and deliver our lives from death"** (Josh. 2:12-13). So the men answered her, **"Our lives for yours, if when we come, and see this scarlet thread in the window through which you let us down, all that remains in the house shall be saved"** (Josh. 2:17-18).

Mary was in such a position to receive the power of a successful vision that the Lord sent an angel to her to let her know she was highly favored and blessed among women, that she would conceive and bring forth a son and call

His name Jesus. She asked, "**How, since that I have not been with a man**" **(Luke 1:34)**. The angel of the Lord said to her, "**The Holy Ghost shall come upon you, and the power of the Highest shall over shadow you**" **(Luke 1:35)**.

The anointing destroys the yoke! God is the anointing; the yoke is our inability to see the anointing. The Word is with God; the Word is God! God demonstrated this by His love for us, in that while we were without strength, Christ died for us so that the yoke of our inability might be destroyed through the anointing. As many as received Him, to them He gave power to become the sons of God, even to them that believe on His name. What you believe is that God did it, not that He was going to do it; this is what the Word means when it says "Now faith is."

How we believe this and receive it determines the results of this experience. These examples I just gave you are the proof of those who believe. Do you believe Jesus Christ is who God says He is? God said, **"Behold, the Lamb that takes away the sins of the world" (John 1:29)**. Do you believe He has already done this? God said, **"This is My Son, in whom I am well pleased" (Matt. 17:5)**. Do you believe this, that God is well pleased with His sons and daughters? These starting points will propel you into position to receive *the power of a successful visionary.*

The Word is anointed because it is with God and proceeds from God.

Every successful vision starts and finishes with God!

"It is finished."

LaVergne, TN USA
29 August 2010
194993LV00005BA/5/P